Fest City

FEST CITY

James Liddy

ARLEN
HOUSE

Fest City

is published in 2010 by
ARLEN HOUSE
an imprint of Arlen Publications Ltd
42 Grange Abbey Road
Baldoyle
Dublin 13
Ireland
Phone/Fax: 353 86 8207617
Email: arlenhouse@gmail.com

Distributed internationally by
SYRACUSE UNIVERSITY PRESS
621 Skytop Road, Suite 110
Syracuse, NY 13244–5290
Phone: 315–443–5534/Fax: 315–443–5545
Email: supress@syr.edu

ISBN 978–0–905223–95–7, paperback

Typesetting ¦ Arlen House
Printing ¦ Brunswick Press
Cover Image ¦ Kyle Fitzpatrick

CONTENTS

13 In South Bend

14 Verses for the Belmullet Festival

15 A Neary's Afternoon

16 July on Either Coast

17 In Raftery's Country

18 For the Inauguration

20 Car Ride with Sean Lucy

21 National Anthem at Wexford Opera

22 On Seeing a Photo of de Valera in a Wheat Field
     with Two Nuns

23 Ó Riordáin's Lament

24 My Lad Oscar

26 I Took My Boyfriend to the Bacon Exhibition
     and Bought a Postcard

27 Career

28 Kirk, A Swain

29 For Kyle

31 Der Vogel

33 I was Invited to Stay in Milwaukee and So I Did

37 Bumper Stickers Etc

43 Fest City New Year's Eve

45 Kubly's Farm, Drinks

46 Aperçus (after being with graduate students)

The Jesuit Boy

49 I   I see you cycling

50 II   What Impression Did Neruda Make on Me?

51 III Are You Sure St. Valentine has a See
     Through Heart?

53 IV Days with John Ashbery

55 V   Jonathan Williams Elegy

57 VI Song of the Gold Bearing Merchant

58 VII Two Dreams

59 VIII Afternoon's White Entrails

61 IX I fish a poem out of …

62 X Jesuit Boy

63 July Bomb

64 May Pole

65 Who's Coming to the Solstice?

66 Maundy Thursday

68 Holy Saturday

69 Them Russians

70 Easter Sunday

71 Feast of the Immaculate Conception

73 In James Liddy's Country
    Michael S. Begnal

80 About the Author

to Jim Chapson, Jeff Sheahan, Paul Vogel

'Inside every heart there are at least two Fest Cities'.

FEST CITY

IN SOUTH BEND

I write from Ivy Court Inn & Suites.
A hot boring kid I wore an ivy leaf
in my lapel in Coolgreany wood,
surrounded by these three other skins,
romance, rebellion, realism.
You foraged each expanding excelsis.
Alright blessed be Avondale tree leaves.

When I was a boy with bread and butter in my heart.

It's been raining all day in this town.
Rain dropped on Hoosiers outside my heart.
Out the hotel window I watch a sign
Irish Import Shop, I get Crunchie bars,
McVities biscuits, and a red button
"I survived an Irish Catholic Childhood".
Eric says "You didn't survive it".

When I was a boy with bread and butter in my heart.

My hot bones are not yet weary
to downtown graduate student Guinness,
but tonight's juice was God in
exile in the chatter and change.
Ivy leaf jumps to Coolgreany wood
to my green core vow. Come God or
fairies, deal us the cards we can play.

When I was a boy with only bread and butter in my heart.

The grey-green bog drives the fire
the wind nudges flares in clouds
nothing is implausible in a place
abandoned from time to time.

Eileen O'Casey talked to me in
a Milwaukee Chinese restaurant:
her parents had the Belmullet hotel,
a chorus girl in London she danced
with the Prince of Wales (Windsor),
"He wasn't much of a man,
in an abandoned moment I asked,
'David, would you like to visit
Belmullet in the Spring incognito',
he smiled upwards at the idea".
Band and dance faded into silence.

Colour parades through the bog like
a pennant, lavender and bog cotton.
If you believe in happiness make
an implausible gesture towards it.

A NEARY'S AFTERNOON

There's Barry Fitzgerald hunched in the corner
with his silver top cane, he buys one drink,
sips the rest of the afternoon from what's
under the silver head—that's Siobhán
McKenna a clutch of theatre owls –
she'll make them rotten with drink,
turn them out later from her Rathgar house.

Salad days in the hostelry of the Golden Fleece.

A nice man comes in, Con Leventhal, tailored,
coiffeured, less Bloom light than Trinity air
either way a street cloud in Dublin. I whisper
how honourable to sell *Ulysses* under
the counter in a pissed Guinness puritan
town – he's off to Paris for Sam's beck and call,
we return to the beautiful nests we have made.

Gold sun down on them as they barge cafe doors.

We say how extravagant it is to choose avatars –
Joyce in his chain-charms of alcohol, Con's
Parisian in colonial chains of less Alcohol.
Clairvoyant modernism costs a lot, we put
on war-weary paint. Padraic Fallon from Wexford
bow-tied joins the table. He doesn't want me
here, who's been telling thespian tales?

Around a corner McDaid's dome under heaven.

JULY ON EITHER COAST

Wicklow/Wexford

Father mother load glasses
four miles from ocean
don't know the names
of the wild flowers on
the golf course fairways

I have to carry the torch
which is never carried
in Ireland into
the bridegroom's chamber

Father's best friend saw
Michael Collins the day
before he was shot
Dionysius shiny revolver

Mother died in Baggot St.
hospital the George Moore
book I brought her stolen
and her money

Her life sort of neo-Moore
I have reluctance to return
to it consternation
at re-entry to womb

Remembering them O Zion
Arklow and Gorey
I hold a mixed drink
in each apparent comedy

It's very dead here there isn't a puff of air
at Knockmaa that is never jaded
the hill that is never bare of mist and leaf
a fountain of fiddles that is now a cottage
behind roses the King of the South Connaught
fairies holds his court of wrists and thighs
Across the road in wooded follied Castle Hackett
the Kirwans croquet and dance
hunt-happy men tune their mallets to an orchestra
or jump over potholes to promenade
the ball holds the beauties of two counties
Venus in bogcotton twilights her low dress
I hang a heart that lies bare on a clothes-line

Here's to you President Robinson
Nostradamus has flown over Dublin
O sweet and thick book your seat.

Here's to you, President Robinson
Seán and Máire, hide from Durcan's
Marxist Unionist kingdom by the bay.

Here's to you, President Robinson
The middle classes' children will
still have to be liberated, Mo Stór.

Here's to you, President Robinson
Flowers and weeds in cemeteries
children will have to write poems.

Here's to you, President Robinson
Priests at the Kerry dances bags packed
for the flight from Shannon to Vegas.

Here's to you, President Robinson
Enflowerment if I dance with my
oul flower I hold gender in my arms.

Here's to you, President Robinson
Song barge into Áras run in Delia
Murphy, a blackbird's throat thirst.

Here's to you, President Robinson
Our Lady of Glendalough, Iseult Gonne,
send mystics into second hand bookshops.

Here's to you President Robinson
Nostradamus has flown over Dublin,
O sweet and thick book your seats now.

CAR RIDE WITH SEÁN LUCY

On 1-94 Seán in the back seat spoke,
"Look at the sky stretching endless —
not the framed sky of our childhood ..."

I remember Seán, 17, white knight
running the rugby ball over the line,
cynosure of faces, sport eye, glad eye ...

Wide horizon, wobbly blue clouds,
prairies supporting herds of thousands,
from his seat Seán sees their incense

and wine: I remember Pindar clapped
you at a refectory afternoon tea table.
In Tom Connolly's car not so long ago

longing to live longing to disappear.

The State dressed up to the nines
rises in solemn eye for the tune
that swells from Gen. Collins's
down-well eyes, his edgy uncertain
mouth, the revolvers both gold
and silver that sway in many hands
and mine, but then I stand up
to feed Redmond's hungry dove.

On Seeing a Photo of de Valera in a Wheat Field with Two Nuns

He lay in bed with God
he wed Him prematurely.

Ó RIORDÁIN'S LAMENT

Not even in *The Irish Times* do they have the gumption
    to cite the word
"homosexual". Dread silences. No lip to lip stop
    permitted in daylight.

I am an inheritor, a butterfly without manliness like a
    lighthouse with
no sea. I occupy a bar cushion I tell you what I would
    like: white rums
on a beach, a file of rent boys through nearby fields
    after rain — rain that
fell on a procession of crosses and Cardinals on a
    Sunday street in Rome.

Seán, it is not a break of love's severe contract to place
    on a young man
a lasting kiss, then somewhat later to kiss eternally
    another young man.

I switch on the light for your 30th anniversary; this
    evening I will
take down from the bookshelf neither Mandelstam nor
    Celan but your
book that has not been translated and I will imagine
    breathing its pores.
On translation, Harnett reset Ní Dhomhnaill, is that a
    living darkness?

I went to Confession, from the priest sensibility, but I
    heard God's lips
whispering, they're better sweeter than the cursing I
    have to do for you.

My Lad Oscar

The fancy boys in the cafes
were worth the fancy drinks
you stuck in your fantasy

Boy mouths on the glasses
spun stories of the absolute
orchestra wind high wind

You were the morning star for
them a performing one for us
your star stuck in your throat

You groaned the addict's pain
in unpublished purple prose
addiction has plans for death

You wore blue lips the last
time I saw you in a dream
of a leper becoming a saint

A Protestant Dublin druid
thing doesn't get to swooning
change title and description

Love is a sin in the scented
sheets of Paris sole city of pride
the Seine a birth control river

Church water tastes champagne
Fr. Dunne Order of Preachers
blessed you by the wallpaper

Fun morning and evening
no fun night of a great event
your soul switched into Salome

this dance floor is beside Jesus

I Took My Boyfriend to the Bacon
Exhibition and Bought a Postcard

The force that though the line drives to the mountain
you exquisite bar and kitchen light in your eyes
owl eyes and mouth in this place
of the assassin of flesh

All song is a mutilation
come and heal this music
in distance this fire
cinders in the mountain now the art museum

Reburnish our flesh
our chests topple into slag
our leaning stuck together kitchen chairs

Now and at the beginning of our wants
so a polished ceremony
you take the Bacon postcard I have
and burn it with a match in adoration on the sidewalk

God woke up as it was done
he spoke as the fire was opened
he called out from the flames
carry your bodies while they still breathe

CAREER

I think I would like
a one candle religion,
in The Poetry Bookshop's foyer

Elizabeth Bowen dazed at
Pound reading by one candle —
candle has not gone out,

us followers of the
Chicago Monroe doctrine
amid Erin's literary brambles —

I parked myself
in Ocean Beach sunrun
poem a writing toy in the distance,

watching cool Jacks
of my heart parade with
their beers under W.P.A. murals.

Bohemian sea-mist I deciphered
I too will sparkle not stutter,
did you change me enough?

Answer: you sure put change in my pocket.

KIRK, A SWAIN

I

I meet a good person
interested in girls
beatifications or

monsoon of descending
sperm finally you
in the rain assert

binding gratification
so I record a failure to
touch as lovers

me weak kneed
you the triste architect
I speak a sentence that

flames in the Kaiser face
on drum on restaurant
wall of Sheboygan Falls

"your sister is a waitress
your friends have no idea
what the smart soul performs"

II

True Swain's Song

"For a boy should bring
toothbrush and toothpaste
into the house of strangers

his morning teeth glitter
at the new table and plate
while his lips hammer out
a dream faded in the night"

FOR KYLE

I attribute your eminence to the five whiskies you
        ordered in Riverwest
as you read *On The Road* the young American's perfect
        afternoon

Your mind has wonderful quavers and so

The book is a joy-ride in the all-seen mirage before
        Planet Mall

My tree leaves outside are French an imported
        nightingale sets amorous
songs which make descent from the branches. You
        smoke in still rain by
the tree under which Eric and I used say goodbye no
        goodbye no one
could hear us bartime tramps

"All one night" Giacometti said "Beckett and I tried to
        make the plaster
tree larger or smaller its branches never seemed right
        and each said to
the other 'maybe'"

Are there friends maybe

Barely thawed raindrops on lovers maybe

DER VOGEL

Beau torso glistens you're a beautiful nowhere
a beautiful everywhere
in the fast lane in two vehicles
passing the bottle out the window
double genies.
Us sirens back at directing email traffic
all those five o'clock shadows, six o'clock.
Happy cursing hour.
To home wine drinkers/readings organizers
a memo:
instead
have Benedict XVI in red slippers
come to read St. Bonaventure's poems
in Latin a short reading.

You met a rabbit on the way home
me a bunny probably a cousin.
Did your one talk on the Wonderland Miss
in the lost glass
mine gave discourse on the White Rabbit Press
let's have a history note
Graham clocked Clayton
I want to blacken Ron's evil eye.
First rabbits of Spring
40 shades of white.
Mother drank a white lady in the Hibernian Hotel
a cocktail gone out of fashion
I remember thinking what if I was a white lady,
up in the tree the owl keeps watch for a white knight
and it's a rabbit
literature is hats and rabbits
love is rabbits and moon hats.

Everywhere they're putting whiskey in birthday cakes
we don't have to google birthday there's James
     Joyce's.
On the flailing spider dance spin
we'll throw webs over each other
wherever their boomerangs on the dance floor
webs in the ancient sense.
Cake in each other's eyes (call it birthday gaze)
at the buffet get into the real spider cake
replica of a Paris bakery.
Party is never over no one leaves
even when birthday goes to heaven
so its candles pray.
Having your cake and
do you give it to the poor?

I thirst said Jesus and Pilate handed him a cup of tea
I pass the cup of plenty to you
with cake.

I WAS INVITED TO STAY IN MILWAUKEE
AND SO I DID

The city always is Rome
The Umpire

I am Aeneas Anchises's son
Europe's son Rome's founder
and so I walked

So what did I do
traded poems with the mermen
at inner sea's edge

So what did it do for me
tall as trees in Lark Park
chaplain to necromancers
fairies merchant seamen

Rome was built late in one night
so happy birthday Mr. Becker
let Lake Michigan merheads
in their speakeasy spill
bathtub vodka for you

Mgr. O'Flaherty retired
WWII scarlet pimpernel
no one drove to Rome airport
to see him off to Cahirciveen
except Mgr. O'Herlihy
St. Gobnait waves to him
in her swarm of bees
Retiree in a cloud lined with
silver crosses no letter ex Rome

Rembert let John XXIII
Benedict XV angel a tray
to you over Lake Michigan
blessed vodka with olives

St. Mary Magdalene
the Virgin Mary at the hour
of my Midwestern death

Hi Catholics I don't trust you
you may have voted Republican
I've no small talk for Judas
nor Herod I take the cup
I like singing hymns in Latin
(*dans le cathedral*)

Instead I grant
David Baptiste Chirot
a *de jure* Renaissance
west of river may they
enunciate it may there be
no offering of it to spouses
You need a new dress I do too
charles henri ford's new outfit
is too southern for us
a whiff of Naples

I wanted to be a nice guy
a colleague but I drank

I gave poetry audiences the benefit
of the doubt of their own existence

I have been ill-used
not by the Muse
but by the poets I grew up with

Vulgar to write
elegies for Michael Hartnett
I knew him

"So you're straight"
"Except in the company
of the poet
turtles kept on making
love in Hiroshima"

Early evening/late evening
to be nice you must be an alcoholic
to be cranky and right you must be alcoholic

Arcady/Summer
People on lakeside rocks smoking weed
maybe the last night they'll have for this

What did I do for Ireland
He had 9 panel pages me 3
read more slowly always
and
Montague's Ireland dead gone
O lecherous O'Connor O'Faolain
and
George Moore in bed with angel
worry about her cooking
and what did I do for me
Bled into sweetheart's heart

What did I do in Milwaukee
besides sing out of tune in temples
I fell for people's life times

I did love and letters
I did love and closing time
I did love and lunch

I did not wait for death
I was driven home
from the bar by a student

Knees under pants regular male knees
glistened in the triangle of tree in wind
moon on porch and Pilsner

In late summer sunshine
let's be sunshine boys

I did
I am still alive
you have so much life
on the porch
we did
no war in our hands
time instead

Hail holy messengers
peace that unRoman thing

BUMPER STICKERS ETC.

Absinthe makes the heart grow fonder
I shall love you until Rimbaud comes back from Africa

The waning moon on the rectory roof the waning
     priest asleep
in his room

I rose again from the meds

I'm for abortion if the fetus wants it

Stars or cakes with sweetness frosting on them

Kind Oracle, reflecting in us

The city came up like a ghost, it was the place we had
     rented

There were sudden flowers: I smelled apparition

Annie, get your dildo

Shave the light over our heads

I held hands as a witness

Kind Oracle, reflecting in us

You got to know how to write sentences, but don't
     keep them isolated

Otherwise promise never to stop talking even
     afterwards

He's a nice guy and a fruit cake

He's a nice guy and a slice of God

My cellphone looks like a chocolate bar I want to eat it

The Empire is gone but I want Pimms Cup 2, 3, 4

Over the hill into the clinic

If I go out with my professor after class will I get aids?

Kind Oracle, reflecting in us

Rooms in the Inn inside God

The right emperor is the emperor of radical clout not
     chic

I'm going out to the airport to have sex with Senator
     Kohl

A ballad is about a person before they become an
     emperor
or a god

A ballad is about someone who might not be a failure

A ballad say is about a man who sits quiet in a corner
who sits in a corner with a grand manner

Here comes God with his begging bowl

At the Pavilion known as the Dating House work for
     peace

Kind Oracle, reflecting in us

Two boys who had nowhere to go but to stars and
    tongues

"In health or in sickness in riches and in poverty", two
    boys
said holding hands on a bed

Till our mothers wake us and we drown

Everything depends on a high school English teacher
who knows what a poem is

The flower sermon should be transferred to the
    classroom
where the teacher asked what a poem is, holds up a
    poem

In youth parents are actual enemies, after they're dead
they become the beloved

Oedipus, it took me 40 years to recover but to you the
    glory

Oscar Wilde's high sad voice, "They're girls, let them
    teach
high school"

On writers the Queen of France remarked, "Put poems
    in their cake"

Kind Oracle reflecting in us

The UWM Creative Writing Program is like the
       Titanic, I got off on a lifeboat.
Paul's comment — dressed as a woman?

The Irish State was founded by Gen. Collins's two
       guns, bullets on the street, penis in London

Collins's guns spoke the two constitutional languages,
       Irish (bullets) English (penis)

The Irish Free State is my state, Yeats's golden warts
       and all

What Ireland needed it got, Collins a man with Yeats's
       golden penis

What America needs is a soccer mum with soccer
       mum legs for President

What we don't need is Joe six pack and Joe blow job

Dogs in the bedroom, plants, fish in the sitting room,
       vegetarian women in the kitchen,
no domestic interior

Send for the leprecauns

Kind Oracle reflecting in us

The leprecauns made me do it, go to church

I became brilliant in old age, I had to wait

Talk is the elixir of life

Two gentlemen not from Verona
Jim Liddy "I liked the Ireland I was born into"
Jim Hazard "I liked the America I was born into"

The secret, love without gender but some eros
    (lifetime to learn)

Are we going to drive down Sperm Road?
Jeff, that's two exits away.
I thought it was only one exit

I'm bored with my own sperm

The death of his poems was kept from the poet

No, Ferlinghetti, one is haunted by bookstores that are
    closed

Kind Oracle reflecting in us

The Messiah is the father of the artist

The Messiah doesn't sit on committees but in Paris
    salons

I walked on air to the pub

I was sweetened by sweat

What angels came along or did they meet me at the
    counter

You rescue angels from poems they don't want to be
    in

An angel has change in his pockets and elsewhere

An angel is a past life flame-up

Driven at last on Highway Heaven

Baudelaire knew one thing, to be a saint

Shall I have eternal delight

On what day did God rest and plant the tree of poems

Colony of welcome stands at the side of the road
which is built not on sand but on a dance floor
enter through the door to lay down your feet
for your friends

This drifting in pubs
makes us Greeks
olives are not mandatory
in the billowy way we wave
syllables slam each other on the counter
interruptions shoot it out

Feast of The Three Bartenders
labeled from year to year
Frank
Ger
and Annie
or "You've got that right"
"You look lovely this evening"
"Come over here darling"
three stars on liberation station
one at the door of Axel's
one in the window of Champion's
one framed on the wall of the Dubliner

What St. Hedwig danced in Listwan's
what the Queen of Sheba danced in Co. Clare
was it Absalom who tap danced outside The Black
        Shamrock
who were the shepherd boys reciting in the Y Not 2

News just in Seamus Heaney danced at
Dublin airport and broke a leg
and Daniel Farsen has stopped dancing
with Francis Bacon's mannikin
and Allen Ginsberg and Bill Burroughs are doing
the Charleston in the National Liquor Bar
I am going to send the photographs to the Tavern
     League

Perhaps we will be partners
we could dance the last one in Nirvana.

KUBLY'S FARM, DRINKS

The window twilight at the first booze of the evening
quarry of cocktails: we shake the ice and argue
Plato's *Symposium*.

A glass in my hand makes an idea beautiful not
        fearful,
I am not so far after the sixties' caresses.
I desire a banana tree with green fruit from there.

The St. Joan Antida teacher I'm with doesn't think
about God's alibis: Steve is classroom-ready,
there ain't no banana juice in his mouth.

APERÇUS (after being with graduate students)

I have not spoken to an American poet
I had not met or thought on before 1985.
Language poets suburbanites dressed as
Bohemians to kill other Bohemians;
we're publication snobs can we resist?
We're up against the gentility principle
good workshop instructors students.
Auden: Get on a diet if you want a job.
Freud: You want to find out the truth
about women, monitor poets' satires.
Marriage: Behaviour men impose on
themselves to be sure to feel nothing.
Keep on falling for a man who doesn't
want you, male beauty is made from this.
Hustle: I'm in college to pick up profs
and liquor cabinets, I don't go to bars.
Ages of Man: Yeats kindergarten 1945-55.
Transitional Kavanagh dancefloor 1955-67.
Neo-clandestine Spicer romancing 1967-85.
Tuned up reincarnations of Joyce 1985-99.
Bustling about Liddy saber rattling 2000—
Moonlit or starlit dome or bar napkin says
friends are flowers bring them more vases.

The Jesuit Boy

I see you cycling in fog and rain and red jacket and
        bike light and street light
Dante in a jacket a half bottle of wine to the good on
        the bike
into nether Riverwest (hipsters dogs) such pour of
        handle bar eyes
a juicy titbit concerning me from the guys in the bar
        under your hat
Who ever said the kindness of heaven centres in a
        courtyard or a garden
drizzle drop night lights on in some of the houses
I almost forgot Police flash lights.
Purgatory the state of mind working as it slides
        through intersections
So what do we think love is some kind of distance
        maybe a gate specifically a door or a door knob
        space that might shine what is this concentrated
        longing that settles from a routine into a nod of
        image
or is it the distance that pushes before me as I try to
        watch it
a bike that smuggles itself off in the dark smaller than
        lamplight
Virgil on handle bars wine in hand
I come to the moment a lover represents a priesthood
        that never passes away
Psalm 44 says the king has greatly desired your beauty

WHAT IMPRESSION DID NERUDA MAKE ON ME?

Being introduced is somewhat an ordeal
the young poet comes to first moon and star
which is in the building of another poet
that body shaped by moon and star.

Knocked around by an aster (this no
Duncan homage but all about you)
it's like being hit by ten Springs in a season.
The sun dances on this is a country for old men

the sun dances on this is a country for young men
the roof of each house of imagery burns
the staircase goes up through it a fire ladder.
Bolaño's *By Night in Chile* sets the stage

what impression did Neruda make on me
the writer asked who was an old Greek god kept
awake by the moon the moon he pushed into
the young man's face a hand rested on the

young man's belt an awful tango record
whispered back at moonlight's end
Neruda my ring master my tango master
my Soviet tank but out of its top jumped beauty.

On the stair's fire top you and I bargain
as night flowers or day flowers demanding
ars poetica not chance so astral lamp-holders
we cast these shadows down on the page:

pent up flat out meteors stray ghosts of meters.

Are You Sure St. Valentine Has a See Through Heart?

Gifts of this Martyr this day:
Winter
Gold

You and I bring these offerings.

I am snowflake, goldflake, vitaflake; Jesus the poor
    boy
who found a flakevoice in the clouds mentioned late at
    night
I set the wrong date for Valentines, in chapel we
    would have
lit inappropriate candles. You and matches. One man
    one candle.

Milwaukee gold room with gold change in our
    pockets. We
squish in snowed shoes to the small altar. Spouses
    lover lover
friend friend, bless our eyes hands tongues in this
    small light.

Till candles out at Mass' end.

No gold
stones thrown at the martyr next day.

Valentine maybe isn't a nice guy, maybe he's not a
    saint at all.
Look at the way he behaved after chapel, asshole
    bartender
in This Is It (This Isn't Anything), asshole smooth
    manager in

Casablanca, Irish asshole customer in three bars.
    Shouldn't
Valentine be demoted or put with the Pagans
    developing to
a sort of local shrine figure in a place like Riverwest?

DAYS WITH JOHN ASHBERY

Days with John Ashbery. A monumental exercise in definitions. Place this screed between the pages of your Douay Bible. Let this be on your desk like a vase of flowers. Then you can select how to go about, how not to go about, *amor* and *poesía*.

I

An Indian student who said he was from Lucknow came up to Ashbery. The poet opened two buttons on the student's shirt to remark, "Look now, pay later". In the crush of Axel's bar we broke up necking between him and a student who said he had slept with Allen. The latter milk fresh from the Seminary was intent on hattricking celebrity poets in one calendar month. The next evening, Wednesday, after Ashbery Bombayed in T. J. Brubakers autographing his art essay in *Newsweek* with what was in his glass, we walked across Downer Avenue to a classroom where he was to preside over Milwaukee writers reading their work. Soon he fell asleep in front of them and snored peacefully. Woken up we climbed to the Kenwood Inn where he took a fancy to my friend Tommy whose tight pants he loudly noticed. They began to embrace. Later Tommy sat in Axel's weeping, "I'm an ordinary guy from Oshkosh, why O why am I so heterosexual when the most famous poet in the world is trying to make me". Later more tears, "Ashbery has asked me to go to New York to be his secretary, I don't know what to do". I heard another student tell the poet, "I have to give you a bad kiss compared to what I give girls".

II

In Dublin Ashbery lunched in The Old Stand and I
think sang a few songs from Victor Herbert. He and
his friend David had come from Portugal, the air
conditioning hadn't worked in Oporto but the poet
commented, "There is always our friend the martini".
He ordered salmon, Paul asked him to sit for a portrait
and offered to give a tour of the gay bars. He
demurred, "I am often bored in such places". John told
a story before he left to pose for Paul in the studio. "I
met Philip Levine who told me he had done an
interview. Levine met Bly who said to him, 'I hear you
said nice things about me'. Levine, 'I said nice things
and not so nice things'. 'What are the not so nice
things?' 'Well I said that you and Gary Snyder were
good poets at the beginning, but then you knew how
poetry was written and your work went down'. Bly
said, 'Yes, that's true about Snyder'".

JONATHAN WILLIAMS ELEGY

I'm labouring this song or
dance near the lake.
I never got in touch with you,
master of small poems still photographs
my sizes. My lament-coated jokes slide
as yours. This desk sent out an Everest
of letters, none to the custodian of our
fates and darlings Dahlberg and Niedecker.

We dance with different someones.
Paul and I took Osip by the sleeves
on to the grass, his soul needs exercise;
Hank Schlau claps, "You and Paul
make me feel Mandelstam without
saying anything directly ... I often feel
Stalin around, watching, shoving the poet
to the ground but Stalin isn't named ..."
We bop up and down to that,
Mr. Williams, you knew the measure.

I could have been a United Nations
sort of person (private life reneged),
but my mother drank and smoked
as I lay her guest in the womb
and so I murmur mad-dark or mad-sweet
secrets to the reader, keep some.
My secret, I wish to dye
Lake Michigan blue, that would be top.
Paul could take my photo in Villa Terrace
too late I want you to snap me as
Lake Michigan turns cobalt blue
(Yeats's colour); it would have gone
to the National Museum of Ireland.

The dance has madcapped itself,
time to announce to the merwaves
Jonathan Williams is dead
a better rhythm picker than Doctor Williams
who played footsie with Uncle Joe. J
stands for Jargon man who was not soft
not at length, a dandy wonder.
We're more than jocund scorekeepers,
we rewrite the scenes. We're three belles,
Bells of the Ball unite: you've nothing to lose
but the ballroom water under your feet.

Apartment's getting cold the bell doesn't work
Jared's car is towed Jamie's hangover is worse
does that stop us laughing even if there's no gold
teeth between us after all we live in a golden hut
in the middle of winter with shelves of gold book
covers a gold label Powers whiskey on the table
sometimes our hands hold each other for so long
like Midas we touch gold frame gold shape gold.

Allen is coming on Saturday on UWM's stage
we're all taking a turn dancing with that corpse
I'm going to ask what he saw in Orlovsky and
you're going to pop this question is it true Frank
didn't make out with you because you're ugly
I'm gonna get into the fight and say just because
O'Hara's Irish doesn't mean you can insult us
(Our Music we sang wild oats not confusion).

Gold fades to Super Tuesday Ash Wednesday
let me thank that which scatters ashes and oats
to our youth blessed be the snow penance on our
foreheads blessed be the delegates on Obama's
brow bless the fire trucks out in blowing drifts
but on Tuesday let's up to vote early and often say
about 1pm if not in voting booths just in booths
ballot rounds cast for the gold standard love party.

Two Dreams

The King of the Fairies was being inaugurated as King
of the Pedophiles on the mound of stones. A lot of
    glitter
and shimmer, ferrets took up dancing. Limestone
    walls
bowed down to sea horses.

Ten miles off in a field by the sea the Son of Man was
putting on the crown of the wild sweet touch, crown
shadow-draped. Grass stalks He stood on were sweet
and juicy. He bowed

and held sweethearts' eyes or hands. Let's hold hands
at day end not to jeopardize sun's rays. My mother's
white roses on the wall are dead: might she wear a
white dressing gown there?

Bring me my banjo of paper talent to play suits of
travel songs to mother memory and to a beloved
down in the town. Dance the set. The kings enter
the stage's opposite doors.

AFTERNOON'S WHITE ENTRAILS

(Scene: Sitting in Henry's Window)

He: Everything is hot and cool at the
      same time.

He: Yes, Spring mixed with Hades.
      Maybe my sister will pass by.

He: Let's go on cocktail alert for her.

He: That would confuse you even more.
      Why don't you keep on picking flowers
      in words?

Pause. Two more vodkas.

He: Will life offer anything as wonderful,
      better than anything out on the street,
      than the hue of your blue shirt, deep blue
      like the shirt my uncle wore marching
      with Yeats.

He: I had to grab something when leaving
      for the Poet Laureate's inaugural.
      It's unwashed.

He: Sparkle, sparkle, little shirt.

He: Maybe my sister will pass wearing a
      blue dress.

He: What's it all about, blue angels?

He: You're going to get separation fever,
     I'll have to come back to break you out.

Pause. Four more vodkas.

I fish a poem out of the Irish Sea.
Prayer in old age
things fall apart
put the golden bullet of love through my brains?

i.e. I don't want any silver bullets.

I'm in the hospital does Nurse Whitman care for me?

Too early for a priest but I remember my Faith:
if thou hast a condo on earth
there is no apartment in a heavenly mansion.

Night prayer:
sex is a nightmare
from which everyone is trying
to awake through falling in love.

Make your way to the hospital through
the Romans in town for Tibersplash
and the Greeks who arrive for Summerfest.

No maidenheads hanging out only love
my thought
begun long ago by the Irish Sea

the alleluia of God he gave me what I wanted
the alleluia of God he brought you and me.

JESUIT BOY

Listen there's a big buzz with me
it's on Radio Global Radio Narcissus
and it's broadcasting glass in hand
inside a springlily Astor St. pub door
outside God's on a street carouse run
in between I struggle a soft loud mouth

You come in saying do you have a fan
we mix Pimm's French pink lemonade
lovers' glasses on a table like a painting
holding hands in a place called Reunion
(an island Baudelaire went A.W.O.L. on)
Me I'm well worth a Mass we're all
worth a Mass (a comment on *Ulysses*)

It's humid I reach to your sticky shirt
Jesuit boy in the world pilgrim to glory

July Bomb

Out of the tilled farm soil of the Germans
out of the castles out of riding horses out of
     universities
out of an aristocratic elite that became an intellectual
     elite
out of dueling clubs out of orchestras ensembles
out of the Jesuit classroom out of the Benedictine
     refectory
out of the melodic lines of Vergil and Catullus
out of Weimar's alleys stuffed with poems
out of top grade plastic explosives out of a timed
     detonator
out of an under the table briefcase in the Wolf's lair
out of the guts of Graf von Stauffenburg, alleluia
     alleluia.

MAY POLE

A blackbird song as ghosts
moved around the May Pole,
"Hitler the Jews the Slavs
a fable crasser than a fable:
how did the beerhallers do it,
how did the dancehallers do it,
how did the Turnerhallers do it,
how did the concerthallers do it,
think of the karma from this".

Who's Coming to the Solstice?

Teachers in training for the posts of messengers.
Religion being more clumsy and awkward than
  morality
the Angelus may not be welcome, as Incarnation is
a debut not an idea: a partying man hands out invites.

Messengers are indefatigable partygoers. The Saviour,
The Curé of Ars who held parties in the Confessional,
Roncalli with his love talk, rock talk, baby talk
Chat-like lyric questions move through the fair.

The Saviour at the wine tasting talked to one
  messenger
more than the others not because he was the youngest
but in order not to show symbolic equal affection.
The teardrops from a Christmas tree, addendum?

MAUNDY THURSDAY

I make myself comfortable
in your arms near Newberry
Blvd grass I know I'm a spy
for a foreign government
it's not Rome it's Washington
I do my work when the night
heats up when the night's fat

There is one thing that makes
me believe love is how Holden
Caulfield or Sal Paradise feel
the lips at the supper table
turn a silver cheek to gold
I don't refer to that shark
hiding in the salmon skin

Pour water the wine lurking
within to the psalm flow
David and Solomon hiding
behind me take questions
if a male and female is
in every body why three person
or four if you include Mary

A body *de jour* could be
trapped in each man or woman
the ancient call of the Greeks
the Church I found today
listens to it so consider the
waters in my jaded face
ghost Jewish writer-kings

They say my father primes
a thousand faces I can
change appearance in moonlight

HOLY SATURDAY

Bring him to the brook
make him drink like a horse
crown him with many crowns
they turn into migraines
wail without a wall

In mixed dawn colours
flustered they arrived
at the tombstone
which strummed like a guitar
blossomed like a buttonhole

awake my soul
and take your medications

Giver of hailstones
cigarettes and antiphons
our death outside the Cross
must be folded inside
the tents we plan

Liberate us from
millenniums and undefined
non-traditional spirituality

THEM RUSSIANS

A country an illness, idleness,
literature was fever

Red skypie at night, delight of
sweet cakewalkers, cakewakers.

Stalin in bed with Pasternak
drunk called him "Anna",

they made out, he launched
his hands on Gorki years ago?

Essenin's hands squeezed.
Isadora Duncan danced through

heads kicked them on the floor
art footballs sheet music for it.

Oh Mandelstam cute, aloof,
God's staring virgin.

EASTER SUNDAY

Arcadia has a cold river
or is it a cool brook
as all saviour all love
melts down our minds
struts hot metal
we don't want to be beguiled
by rising too fast
though the name in the Book
reads the name in my heart
the name is on the circus poster
circus man whisper a line of
a song while we're in the pews
Two things saints have to
pray to tombs under Rome
the vine in the numinous
The New Testament is at least
as large as O'Hare field
but probably no bigger
than a farmer's field
that stretches in front of us
wind in the windy city
raspberry and strawberry
cocktails with the likes
of Joan of Arc Woody Guthrie

This was what I was going to add when you had to go
    back to your Supervisor.

I was talking with the Virgin Mary and she asked if I
    needed a lawyer to advise
me on domestic matters. I thought for a moment,
    maybe she's a lawyer as she
comes from a good Jewish family. She saw my
    thought, smiled, and said she
was a poet. She writes in Hebrew and English. She
    said to me, "Why aren't you
nice to Jeff on the phone, he's a poet too", but she was
    joking again (thank God
for that). So now I put an imaginary blue (Mary's
    colour) envelope around this.

IN JAMES LIDDY'S COUNTRY

Michael S. Begnal

It's been two years since James Liddy's death. But with *Fest City* I return to Liddy's country, as I often do through reading his work. Liddy's country is a wondrously singular place. It is not Ireland, as much as it often resembles it, and it's not America either, as much as it resembles the latter as well. But that's one of the reasons why I like Liddy's country so much – because it reminds me of these familiar places, and yet it's something distinctly else. Liddy's country is poetry. A poet has to make his own country. His country is self-created, or recreated, through the medium of poetry. To put it another way, the poet creates himself through poetry. I'm sure that something like this has been said before, but if ever there was a poet who exemplified this dynamic, it was Liddy. In fact, in many ways, his life and his poetry were virtually indistinguishable. Both his everyday speech and his written work, at least by the time I got to know him, seemed to me to occur on a similar plane; it all seemed to come from the same place, from his own country of poetry. His letters too were like poems, with gossip and tidbits of news included. And his poems sometimes read like letters (often they are addressed to particular people), delivered via the Muse from his mind to the page stamped with international postage.

Reading back the preceding paragraph, I suddenly wonder if it ought to be revised or perhaps scrapped altogether. Sometimes it's uncomfortable to talk about things like 'the Muse' and 'the poet' without some kind of irony, without quotation marks. It might seem silly or self-important. But still I like the paragraph as it is because it says what I want it to say, despite my petty ambivalence about the way it needs to be phrased, and so I'll leave it in. As Jack Kerouac writes (both ironically and ultimately sincerely) in 'MacDougal Street Blues', 'But I can't write, poetry,/ just prose// I mean/ This is prose/ Not poetry/ But I want/ To be sincere ...' In that poem, Kerouac too was trying to get at a kind of meaning that may come off to some as laughable – it's an attempt to be sincere in a society that instead values its poses, its triviality, ignorance, the ersatz. James Liddy loved Kerouac, and he loved sincerity. And when all is said and done, so do I. Being of a later generation, I think it's possible to accept popular culture and also be a serious poet, but Liddy did not even own a television. That's how serious he was (by which I do not mean that he lacked a sense of humour).

In reading *Fest City*, I return again to Liddy's country. As I said, sometimes it looks a lot like Ireland, especially the Ireland of his youth, though it may not accord exactly with an objective Ireland of the present day. But, we are talking about poetry and not prose. I mean James wrote poetry, not documentary newspaper articles. Sometimes he wrote of Ireland in a way that I would characterize almost as imagist in the classic sense, a technique by which, as in an imagist poem, a sudden insight is achieved in the stark observance of a visual scene: 'The grey-green bog drives the fire/ the wind nudges flares in clouds/ nothing is implausible in a place/ abandoned from time to time' ('Verses for the Belmullet Festival'). In 'July on Either Coast', a vision of Liddy's parents pouring drinks, set against wild flowers on a golf-course fairway, leads to the statement, 'I have to carry the torch/ which is never carried/ in Ireland into/ the bridegroom's chamber' – this weird juxtaposition of images and ideas is a hallmark of much of Liddy's work, and it features here in this, the first of three collections he prepared for posthumous publication. What exactly does it mean that the speaker must 'carry the torch which is never carried in Ireland into the bridegroom's chamber'? Again, I don't think we can translate it into precise prose, but the epithalamium is one of Liddy's favorite forms. And certainly one of his great preoccupations in his work is with the figure of his mother (who was incidentally American). I'm no psychoanalyst, so make of all this what you will.

Liddy was also, of course, gay, and homosexuality was not always something that played well in traditional, old-fashioned Ireland. Now it's largely a different story there (or at least as much as it is anywhere that's not, say, Africa or Iran), but as the poem 'Ó Ríordáin's Lament' (written on the 30th anniversary of the poet Seán Ó Ríordáin's death) demonstrates, the conservative homophobia of the Ireland that Liddy grew up in was something he bristled at: 'Not even in *The Irish Times* do they have the gumption to cite the word/ "homosexual". Dread silences. No lip to lip stop permitted in daylight'. (Perhaps this partly explains why, as Liddy once told me, 'America is to the Irish writer, or should be, a form of liberation'.) In contrast to the oppressive attitudes of an earlier Ireland, as we see in *Fest City* and for that matter all of his work, Liddy is quite happily out. But while the particularities of gay life are of course important, in the larger sense his poetry is nothing if not simply an affirmation of love. His poetics is a poetics of human relationships, not unlike

Ó Ríordáin's. While Ó Ríordáin is in many ways a spiritual poet and a nature poet, the final line of his 'Oileán agus Oileán Eile' is the statement, 'Raghad anonn ag cabaireacht sa tsaol', translated by Muiris Ó Ríordáin as, 'I will go gossiping in the taverns of life'. This line seems to me to sum up James Liddy perfectly. We can say that he is Irish, American, gay, Catholic – all of the by-now-usual labels cited when discussing his work – but ultimately he is best understood as a poet who goes gossiping in the taverns of life.

So reading *Fest City*, I track place-names of streets and neighbourhoods and follow James around Milwaukee. I imagine him riding through the city, either with friends or maybe among unknown fellow passengers on the bus, moving along wide boulevards. James often took the bus, and when I visited him in Milwaukee in 2004 we took the bus together. Other times we were driven around by his friend and one-time student Keith Gaustad (who appears in this same capacity in the poem 'German-American Driving', from the 2006 collection *On the Raft with Fr. Roseliep*, and who co-authored a 2004 chapbook with Liddy titled *Songs on the Plane Carrying Hess from Germany*). A few of the poems here in *Fest City* refer to the Riverwest neighbourhood of James's adopted city. Riverwest is something of a bohemian, hipster neighbourhood. It's an area where artists, musicians, and students live cheaply, where there are good bars and a renowned independent bookshop (Woodland Pattern). At other times James preferred the more upscale surroundings of Astor Street, with its hotels and hotel bars, where one could drink in grander grandeur, so to speak. James's favorite Milwaukee bars, past and present, are celebrated in *Fest City*, and especially in the poem 'Fest City New Year's Eve' –

there's Axel's (which featured in much of Liddy's mid-period work, but has apparently since gone downhill), Champion's (a sports bar which I hear is therefore preferable during the day), The Dubliner (now closed), Listwan's (an inspirationally dingy dive bar), the County Clare (a spacious Irish pub on Astor Street, where I once had lunch with James), the Y Not II (another dive bar), and the old Black Shamrock pub.

With such a litany of drinking establishments, with such a celebration of bohemianism, it might seem almost contradictory at first that Liddy's country is also partly composed of the Rome of the Catholic Church. While the reader could reasonably see *Fest City* as an homage to the city of Milwaukee, to the relationships Liddy has forged there, its bars, or to Ireland, or even as a celebration of a homosexual worldview, or to all of these at once (there is really no compartmentalization in his work), Liddy's Rome of the mind is never far beneath the surface. Indeed, as he writes in 'I Was Invited to Stay in Milwaukee and So I Did', 'The city always is Rome …' For Liddy, his bohemianism is in no way at odds with his vision of Christ and Catholicism. As far back as his long poem *Corca Bascinn* (1977), he writes that 'the fun we have in the bar is our/ Mass …' In the present volume, this attitude is expressed in 'A Neary's Afternoon': 'Around a corner McDaid's dome under heaven' – with McDaid's pub, Dublin, here taking on the role of cathedral. Of course, the bar or the pub is also about people coming together for a common purpose, as is a Mass; each is a communion of sorts, be it with a lower-case 'c' or a capital 'C'. In 'Fest City New Year's Eve', Liddy creates his own Catholic feast day, the 'Feast of the Three Bartenders'. And he is not merely trying to be cheeky, despite his obvious sense of humour. However, his Church is clearly not the Church of judgmental conservatism. In 'I Was Invited to Stay in Milwaukee', he writes, 'Hi Catholics I don't trust you/ you may have voted Republican'. Politically, Liddy was a progressive and was a supporter of Obama, and lived just long enough to see him elected. But he was by no means a follower of some kind of fluffy, do-it-yourself, New-Age version of Catholicism. As he entreats in 'Holy Saturday', 'Liberate us from/ millenniums and undefined/ non-traditional spirituality'. James was serious about his Catholic faith. When I visited him in Milwaukee in 2004 there was a statue of St. Barbara in his apartment, which I believe he obtained from a desacralized church.

Now James Liddy is gone, but the country that he created (to continue the metaphor) lives on through his work and through his influence on a generation of younger poets too numerous to list here. There is an affecting awareness of death looming in some of the poems in *Fest City*, but they are never maudlin, even when he writes in the sequence titled 'The Jesuit Boy', 'Prayer in old age/ things fall apart/ put the golden bullet of love through my brains? [...] I'm in the hospital, does Nurse Whitman care for me?' Instead, these poems are affirmations of life and poetry – even in the hospital there are references to Yeats ('things fall apart') and Whitman, while what might seem like a vague suggestion of suicide instead alludes, I think, to the recurring theme of 'gold' in Liddy's own work. Brian Arkins has pointed out that Liddy's gold is redolent of the gold of Yeats's 'Sailing to Byzantium' (which Yeats likened to 'God's holy fire'). If death must come, Liddy seems to be saying, then let it be like God's holy fire. But these poems were written before death, and their message is to carry on living until it's no longer possible, to sip every last drop. The final line or epiphany of 'I Took My Boyfriend to the

Bacon Exhibition' is that God calls out, 'carry your bodies while they still breathe'. And while we still breathe we must continue to go gossiping in the taverns of life. The party isn't over until it's over. In fact, as James puts it in 'Der Vogel', 'Party is never over no one leaves/ even when birthday goes to heaven ...' So, while James may be gone in one sense, those of us holding this book in our hands, reading it, know that he has not really left us.

Michael S. Begnal has published the poetry collections *Ancestor Worship* (Salmon, 2007), *Mercury, the Dime* (Six Gallery Press, 2005), and *The Lakes of Coma* (Six Gallery Press, 2003). He was editor of the Galway-based literary magazine *The Burning Bush*, and also edited *Honeysuckle, Honeyjuice: A Tribute to James Liddy* (Arlen House, 2006). His next collection, *Future Blues*, is forthcoming from Salmon in 2011.

James Liddy was born in Lr. Pembroke St., Dublin, in 1934. His parents hailed from the cities of Limerick and New York. He lived in Coolgreany, County Wexford, intermittently from 1941 to 2000. His books include *Blue Mountain* (Dolmen), *A Munster Song of Love and War* (White Rabbit), *Corca Bascinn* (Dolmen), *Baudelaire's Bar Flowers* (Capra/White Rabbit), *Collected Poems* (Creighton University), *Gold Set Dancing* (Salmon, 2000), *I Only Know that I Love Strength in My Friends and Greatness* (Arlen House, 2003), *On the Raft with Fr. Roseliep* (Arlen House, 2006). *Wexford and Arcady* (Arlen House, 2008) and *The Askeaton Sequence* (Arlen House, 2008).

He was a Professor in the English Department at the University of Wisconsin-Milwaukee for many years, where he taught creative writing and Irish and Beat literature. *James Liddy: A Critical Study* by Brian Arkins was published by Arlen House in 2001 and the widely acclaimed *Honeysuckle, Honeyjuice: A Tribute to James Liddy*, edited by Michael S. Begnal, appeared in 2006.

The first volume of his memoir, *The Doctor's House: An Autobiography* was published by Salmon in 2004, with volume two, *The Full Shilling*, appearing from Salmon in 2009.

He passed away on 5 November 2008 following a short illness, leaving behind completed manuscripts for this collection and a final one which will be published in Spring 2011.